Read this simple book and see how you can easily turn your business idea into a reality in as simple as ABC.

This simple but very essential book was inspired by how easily I found it to start my own business by following the same simple steps and principles.

Table of Contents

A. Chapter One - A business Idea 4
B. Chapter Two - Start Trading 13
C. Chapter three - Managing your Business Finances 20
D. Chapter Four -- Policies, Processes, Controls and Procedures 53
E. Chapter Five - Regulatory Filings & Requirements. 57
F. Chapter Six - Compliance.. 69
G. Chapter Seven – Accountant 70

I dedicate this book to my mother, my husband and my children who have supported me through this challenging time.

A. Chapter one - A business Idea

Hooray! You have a fantastic business idea…. What next?

Do you have a:

- Business name;

- Business plan;

- Business website?

    - Wix is the most recommended global website template provider
    - Speak to a professional about Search Engine Optimization (SEO). This will
    - Determine how quickly your website can be found on the search engine

- Business cards;
    - Most recommended providers; Moo and Vista in the UK. There are other
    - Competitively priced global providers do your search.

- Insurance

- It is highly recommended that you take out all the relevant insurances before you start trading. This will cover you and your business against unforeseen misfortunes. Below is a list of recommended insurance;

- Public Liability Insurance; examples of providers in the UK are;

  - AXA
  - AVIVA
  - Direct Line
  - Small Business Insurance
  - In other regions please look for competitive providers

- Product Liability

- Professional Indemnity Insurance – If you give advice in any shape or form, you have to have PII;

- Employers Liability Insurance;

- Operating licenses? – Speak to the local Authorities or your professional body to know which licenses you need to legally carry out your business operations.

Got a marketing strategy?

Free is cheap! Have you tried the free and cheap marketing options first?

Here you go.

- Word of mouth.
- Business cards – a must have.

- Social media like:
- Facebook;
- LinkedIn – This is better if you are providing professional services;
- Twitter;
- Instagram;
- You Tube;
- Myspace;
- What's Up;
- Periscope.
- If B2C cold calling – be clear, pleasant and concise. You only have the first 30 seconds to make an impact
- Surveys – You can use "www.SurveyMonkey.co.uk" website to design your surveys.
- Sponsorship: Local Radio Station – Target their promotional periods where you can get an ad aired for free or at a discount.
- T-shirt or other accessories.

- Local newspapers – Metro
- Networking event – BNI www.Meetup.com.

At this stage, it is safer to stay away from expensive adverting and marketing strategies.

Got your Start-up Capital?

Terms like seed capital or seed money are often used in reference to start-up capital.

Seed capital is the initial cash or funds used to start a business.

Again free is cheap….. And keep it simple….

- Do you have any savings?
    - This should be your first choice of capital but do not invest all your savings just in case you need something to fall back onto.

- Have you tried friends and family?
    - But a word of caution, only get cash or loans from family and friend who share the same vision as you, for the business.

    - The terms of payment, if it is a loan should be clear and agreed upon before funds are advanced. If cash is given in exchange for a share of the business, it is advisable that a professional is consulted to advise on the terms and the agreement to be signed.

- Grants – bodies that may support your business idea for Example;
    - The Prince's Trust and CDFIs (Community Development Financial Institutions)

- Start-up Loans – The less money you want to borrow the easier it is to get the loan.
    - Try www.startuploans.co.uk/.

- Crowdfunding – This is a new way of raising finance for your start-up.

- With crowdfunding, members of the public can pool their resources to help you hit your fundraising target, investing anything from £10 each.
- Check http://startups.co.uk/crowdfunding/.
- Credit cards – If your start-up capital is £700 - £1,500, your business can benefit from credit cards like the following as long as you ensure that the minimum payment is maintained every month.

    - Vanquish
    - Capital One
    - Aqua

- You can also get a bank loan from your bank or any of the high street banks like Metro. However with this kind of funding, you will be required to make repayments immediately which may be difficult. This method should be considered as last resort but you should ensure that your business can afford the repayments otherwise; you risk bad credit and CCJs.

B.   Chapter Two - Start Trading

You now have your capital and you are ready to start trading.

Hang on a minute!!!!!!!!!!!!!!!!! What type of Business structure are you going to trade under?

In the case of the United Kingston, Is it……..?

Sole Trader

- Here you will be on your own. You and your business are one and the same from both the tax and legal perspective.
- You are personally responsible for the Business and any debts it incurs.
- All the profits you make (which is the sales minus the costs) until 5 April every year have to be declared on your annual self-assessment as your income. The online deadline for this submission is 31 January every year.
- You must pay national insurance and income tax on this income at standard income tax rates.

- Once you start trading, you have to inform HMRC that you are in operation and that you are self-employed for tax purposes.

Partnership

- Two heads are better than one! This arrangement is similar to sole trader the only difference is that there are two of you instead of one owner.

- Partners own a specific percentage of the profits and liabilities, therefore each must pay taxes on the percentage they own.

- Like in the case of a sole trader, each partner's share of profits is treated as their income for tax purposes.

Limited Liability Partnership

- This is when you choose "to tango" / partnership but also have characteristics of a limited company.

- You are unlikely to use this company structure. It is mostly used by professional services like Accountants, Lawyers and architects.

Limited Company

- The Business has to be registered at Company's house. Once it is incorporated, it is given a registration number. For registration in the UK please view the following link; https://www.gov.uk/register-a-company-online.

- The Business is a separate legal entity.

- It must have certain legal documents that govern what business it is involved in.

- This business is owned and controlled by those who own its shares. Once the company has been incorporated you can choose to allocate the shares to any number of people or you can choose to keep all the shares.

- However, a Limited company comes with more administration work like filing Annual returns and Annual accounts to Company's House and Annual Accounts and Corporation Tax to HMRC. Do not worry about this

…. *Your Accountant will take care of it!*

Advantages of Limited Companies

- Reduced risk – the debts (liabilities) of the company are separate from that of the owner. This reduces the risk when the business fails to meet its financial commitments.

- Tax efficiency – The Director has the ability to receive income in form of both salary and Dividends.

- Limited companies portray a more professional image of the business.

Have you made up your mind which company structure suits you and your business?

Great!!!!

C. Chapter three - Managing your Business Finances

Again Simple is better!

Sales

The power of generating sales lies in knowing your product like the back of your hand, talking about your product with passion, knowing your target market, understanding the needs of your customers and where gaps in meeting these needs lay and finding and exploiting your business' unique selling factor.

Tips on how to sale your product

- Get your pricing right.

    o Get your pricing right. You have to choose a "Goldilocks Zone" where price is not too high or too low. Make sure you retain a reasonable gross margin (Sales minus cost of sales). This margin will help you pay for your overheads and also retain a profit. At this stage there is no need to sale when you cannot cover your costs.

- Sell the benefit

    o Tell your customer what makes your product different. Ways to do this

- - Cost – you have to price your product better than the competition
    - Quality
    - A combination of the two
  - When selling emphasize the benefit of the product to the customer and not how your product is, compared to competition. However when marketing you can make comparison by highlighting features of your product

- Listen to your customer
  - For example people who live in rural and suburban areas often buy in larger quantities because they have larger families or need more goods to keep their own small

businesses stocked and running. The customer may at times defy logic, but they are always right. Listen to them

- Think outside the box

    o The marketing landscape has dramatically changed over the year. Years back, there were no search engines or social media platforms. There was no internet as we know it. Now, startups can utilize a crowd of free, online marketing techniques that are both creative and effective. For example, you can use online video marketing, social media, blog influencers, crowdsourcing, competitions, content marketing, thought leadership and more.

- Market your product before it is ready;

    o Some businesses wait until their product is perfect before they do any marketing or awareness campaigning. That can be a costly mistake. Many businesses expect to sell their product as soon as it's ready. But if no one knows about it, then demand will start at zero until you undergo a marketing campaign to build brand awareness for potential customers.

    o It's better to do pre-emptive awareness campaigning, even if it's minimal, to let potential customers know your product is coming. You can sell the benefit before the product has arrived. This way, when the product is ready, so are customers!

- Test fast, Fail fast

    o Marketing that you can't measure is failed marketing. Sure, you may spend money to do some advertisement, and you may even see an uptick in sales around the same time you ran the ads. But how can you be sure what you spent on ads correlates with sales? Maybe it was something else altogether. Maybe there is a natural, seasonal uptick for what you sell that will go away in a month.

- If you're going to commit time and money to a marketing campaign, make sure you can measure the results. Set up ways to track conversions that stem from each marketing campaign. Also, run multiple types of marketing campaigns in distinct, small batches. This will allow you to compare marketing channels and see which perform best. Toss out the ones that don't work and keep those that do.

- Advertise through several channels

  - As mentioned above, it's good to test multiple marketing channels and ideas to see what works best. Often, it's not any one thing but a combination of all of the above.

When your customer hears you on the radio, sees you in a search engine result, and then finds you mentioned in a blog they like (content marketing), they start to accept your brand as a solid, dependable, known entity. They may not have the need for your product or service immediately, but when they do, it will be your name that comes to mind instead of a competitor's.

- It is always time for PR (Public Relations)
    - When you do traditional advertising, it's your marketing material selling your product. When you do PR, or have a member of the press or a media house that covers your

industry talk about you, its brand building and endorsement.

- Some people call it landing-page flair or credibility building, but, if your company is featured in *Mashable* or *The Wall Street Journal*, you'd be silly not to put that paper's name on the front of your company's website. Even if your company was only mentioned by way of a quote from your CEO, you are still "as mentioned in *The Wall Street Journal*." When customers see that publication's name next to your company's name, it builds credibility.

- Even little PR wins, like local news or blogs, add up. And, unlike most traditional marketing, PR endures far beyond the dates of the advertising campaign. Good PR can do a lot for your credibility and brand awareness.

- Give customers a place to talk to or about you
    - Good or bad, you want to know what your customers are saying. If you don't provide your customers with a place to complain or praise you, it makes it look like their thoughts and opinions don't matter. Remember, even if a customer comes to you and is furious, that's a great opportunity for you to publicly show how willing you are to right a wrong, or make a customer feel valued -- which is PR gold!

- o By providing a place on your website site for this kind of exchange to happen, you can address the issue and control a portion of that narrative. The alternative is that your customer goes to a third-party site and complains where you can't address the issue nor tailor an edited response.

- Reward customer Loyalty

  - o Your customers are your sales department.
    - Word-of-mouth testimonials and customers who are brand advocates are better than any sales team you could put together. So, continuously

reward customers with competitive pricing, incredible customer-support and automatic updates to enhance the software.

- Now that you have closed a sale

    o If it is for a service, ensure you have a signed contract with clear Terms of Engagement and Standard Terms of Business.

    o If it is for products, ensure that the purchasing company raises a purchase order as a sign of commitment.

    o Take 50% or more of the price of the service upfront.

- Ensure that an invoice for the remaining balance is raised on completion and terms of payment clearly indicated on the invoice. Remember to quote the purchase order or work order number on the invoice.

- It is safer, cheaper and quicker to send an electronic copy of your invoice to your supplier than mailing it.

- Sales generation is very important for the survival of any business. Great customer care is invaluable in making sure that you have high customer retention.

- As well as getting new sales / customers, make sure that the recurring ones are kept happy

- Think about ways of rewarding your customers for example coupons, draws, discounts etc.

- Log your successful sales in an excel spreadsheet similar to the one below.

Sales Register

Customer Name	Invoice No.	Purchase Order No.	Date	Total Cost	Total Price	Payt on Acnt	Outstand'g Bal	Payt due date

- Keep a log of your potential sales and show the level of completion.

Customers in the Pipeline

Customer Name	Product	Introduction Stage 10%	Conversion	Negotiation stage 50%	Final stage	Completion 100%
Mg Stores	Coffee					
Starbucks	Ground					

- If you are providing services, get into a habit of reviewing your customer contracts on a regular basis to ensure that the dates are still valid.

- If you're selling products check associated purchase orders on a regular basis to ensure that deliveries are covered by the purchase order.

- Now that your business is generating sales, how is your cash position?

Cash Flow

In simple terms, there is no point in generating sales if you do not get cash.

- Cash management is one of the most important things in a business start-up or in any business for that matter.

- Avoid providing any services or parting with any products without receiving cash for B2C or a substantial percentage of the value of the product upfront for B2B contracts.

- Record every penny spent using business funds and every receipt. Get into a habit of filing all receipts and invoices. Once you get into a habit of doing it, it will come naturally. Most importantly it will save you lots of Professional fees if you have to hire an accountant to file your tax returns.

- Avoid unnecessary expenses …. Do you really need to rent an office or you can use one of your rooms at home for now? Do you really need to hire an employee or you can get away with a contractor?

- Check your business bank account every morning.

- During the first few months of trading, get into a habit of having a weekly cash flow. That way, you are not caught off guard when important payments like HMRC fall due. You will also be in a better position to manage your suppliers' expectations.

- Negotiate longer supplier payment terms.

- You can also consider invoice financing. Invoice financing is where a third party agrees to buy your unpaid invoices for a fee. Invoice financiers can be independent, or part of a bank or financial institution. There are two types:

    o Factoring - also known as 'debt factoring' - usually involves an invoice financier managing your sales ledger and collecting money owed by your customers themselves. This means your customers will know you're using invoice finance.

- When you raise an invoice, the invoice financier will buy the debt owed to you by your customer.

- They make a percentage of the cost (usually around 85%) available to you upfront.

- They then collect the full amount directly from your customer.

- Once they've received the money from your customer, they make the remaining balance available to you.

- You'll have to pay them a discount charge (interest) and fees - the amount depends on which invoice financier you use.

- **Invoice Discounting** - With 'invoice discounting', the invoice financier won't manage your sales ledger or collect debts on your behalf. Instead, they lend you money against your unpaid invoices - this is usually an agreed percentage of their total value. You'll have to pay them a fee.

- As your customers pay their invoices, the money goes to the invoice financier. This reduces the amount you owe, which means you can then borrow more money on invoices from new sales up to the percentage you originally agreed.

• You'll still be responsible for collecting debts if you use invoice discounting, but it can be arranged confidentially so your customers won't find out.

Advantages

- Both kinds of invoice financing can provide a large and quick boost to your cash flow.

Advantages of factoring include:

- the invoice financier will look after your sales ledger, freeing up your time to manage your business;

- they credit check potential customers meaning you are likely to trade with customers that pay on time;

- they can help you to negotiate better terms with your suppliers.

Advantages of invoice discounting include;

- it can be arranged confidentially, so your customers won't know that you're borrowing against their invoices;

- it lets you maintain closer relationships with your customers, because you're still managing their accounts.

Disadvantages

- Some disadvantages of invoice financing are that:

    - you'll lose profit from orders or services that you provide;

- invoice financiers will usually only buy commercial invoices - if you sell to the public you might not be eligible;

- it may affect your ability to get other funding, as you won't have 'book debts' available as security.

o If you use factoring:

- Your customers may prefer to deal with you directly.

- It may affect what your customers think of you if the invoice financier deals with them badly.

- Instead of paying for that equipment upfront, have you considered Leasing or Hire purchase? Explore options that will help you avoid huge cash outlays because at this stage, you need all the cash you can get your hands on. Using credit options will help you build and improve your business' credit score.

- Get your business a Sum-up Credit Card Reader so that you can take card payments from your customers anytime anywhere.

- Please visit www. sumup.co.uk

- Above all, cash discipline is very important. Although it is technically your business, you must not use business money for personal use. If you do, you must declare it as part of your personal income. In a Limited company, this may attract P11Ds.

Cost of sales.

- These are the total costs that are used to create a service or a product which you have sold. For example if you are selling coffee, your cost of sales is going to be calculated as beginning coffee inventory plus any purchases of coffee you have made during that period minus remaining coffee at the end of the period. Cost of sales will appear near the top of the income statement and will be subtracted from net sales to give you the Gross profit.

- Cost of sales is very important in the performance of the business.

- This is because it will determine your business's ability to design, provide, and purchase goods and services at a reasonable price.

- Ensure that you negotiate reduced prices from your suppliers.

- Push for longer payment terms. This way you can use the funds to grow your business rather than pay your suppliers. However ensure that once you have agreed payment terms with your suppliers, you honor them otherwise you risk defaults and ruining credibility and trust.
- Before you enter into a supplier contract especially one where you are required to pay some money upfront, make sure that you have:

- Carried out due diligence on the supplier;
- You have read all the terms and condition, including the tinny prints and are comfortable with them.

- If you have regular suppliers who have rolling contracts (contracts that automatically get renewed), ensure that you review the terms of these contracts on a regular basis especially the section relating to pricing.

Business Overheads

- Business overheads are those costs incurred excluding any costs that are required to create products and services, for example direct labor and material costs during the normal operation of the business.

- o They include all costs that do not directly generate revenue but are required to maintain the business. These costs include expenses like professional fees, taxes, rent, rates, staff salaries, advertising, depreciation, utilities, insurance, interest, repairs and maintenance, office supplies, travel and so on.

Even if you have a very big gross profit margin, the way you manage your business' overheads will determine whether you are a profitable business or not. Keep a very close eye on your business overheads!

- o Negotiate discounted prices with your suppliers.

- Look out for invoices from bogus suppliers.
- Efficiently manage the utilization of your resources. For instance ensure that your employees are motivated and fully utilized- look out for employees who spend half the time on the phone, internet or coffee breaks!

- Review each of your bills or invoices to ensure that you are not billed for services you have not utilized. Pay specific attention to utility providers
    - like gas and electricity. It is not unusual for their bills to be based on estimated figures. Make sure that they have the actual meter readings.

- Avoid penalty charges like late payment of PAYE, VAT, late submissions.

- These are unnecessary costs that drain your cash flow.

- Get into a habit of knowing all the overheads you have to pay out each month so that if there is any discrepancy you can easily pick it up.

- Do not incur an overhead unless you have too.

- All in all, whenever you have to pay out any money, check to make sure that you completely understand why and that you have to.

Budget

Do you have a budget or cash flow forecast?

- A Budget is a benchmark based upon which you will measure your business' progress or performance. It will include your yearly projected sales, cost of sales and overheads. It provides a motivation to work hard to either meet or beat the projected sales or net profit.

- Review your budget every month to ascertain where your business is at compared to the budgeted or forecasted figures. It is dangerous to wait until the end of the year to review your numbers; it may be too late to exploit missed opportunities.

    o Your budget has to be SMART

- Specific

- Measurable

- Attainable

- Realistic

- Time bound otherwise it will be meaningless to use it as a benchmark.

Treasury Management

- Has your business been making so much money that you have a lot of cash sitting on your business current account?

    o If yes... that is not a good idea. You should make sure that your money is earning you more money every time. Call your bank and put the cash you will not need on a treasury deposit account... It will earn you some interest.... Not a lot, but it will be better that leaving it on your current account.

- o Ensure that you review your cash flow forecast on a weekly basis. This helps you to determine how much cash you will need every week so that you can deposit the rest on a treasury account to earn you some interest.

- o As part of treasury management, ensure that you take advantage of any early settlement discount offered by your supplier. This is when your suppliers offer to give you a discount on the value of the invoice if you settle the invoice within a specific period. This will save you some money.

D. **Chapter Four - Policies, Processes, Controls and Procedures**

- In order for your business to be successful, it has to have systems in place. There should be a set of rules to follow when tasks are being completed and there should be clear instructions to show everyone how each task should be completed.

Do you know that these words are different?

Policies

- These are the guidelines that drive the process and procedures in the business. For instance it could be your business policy that all payments are made by the Director.

Procedure

- These are the detailed steps that are required to perform an activity for instance payment of suppliers, within the process.

Process

- This is a set of interrelated activities that interact to achieve a result. For example when considering your supplier payment approval process, you have to look at the process from when you receive the invoice to the point when you actually pay it. How do you determine if this particular invoice should be paid?

- Strong financial controls will not only help you prevent and detect fraud but they will also help you detect genuine mistakes in the accounting and management reporting.

- Your company should have set processes by which specific tasks are carried out. For example there should be clear;

    o Supplier payment process / Accounts payable system.

    o Cash payment system

    o financial reporting process

- Customer invoicing process
- Receipts processing process
- Purchasing process
- Credit collection process
- Payroll process

* All key functions in your business should have policies for instance.

- Travel policy
- Recruitment policy
- Procurement policy / purchasing policy
- Marketing policy

- o Employee expenses policy

- Check that your processes are not broken and that all procedures are followed when completing tasks. This will help you to minimize risks like paying bogus invoices.

- In order to minimize risk within the business ensure that all processes, controls and procedure are reviewed on a regular basis.

E. **Chapter Five - Regulatory Filings & Requirements**

- These are specific to the United Kingdom. Review your local regulatory requirements.

UK Sole Traders or Limited company?
- While a limited company is taxed as a separate entity from its owners and

Directors, sole traders (and partners in partnerships) and their businesses are taxed as one and the same entity.

- If your business is a limited company it will be subject to Corporation Tax on their annual profits but its director must file an annual self-assessment return to cover any income they have taken from the business.

- If you are a sole trader or partner in a partnership, you will be taxed via self-assessment system every year. You will also have to pay tax and National Insurance Contribution on your business profits after deducting expenses.

Self-Assessment Tax Returns

- Once you have registered as self-employed, you will be sent a self- assessment notice with a UTL number at the end of each tax year which runs from 6 April to 5 April every year.

- If you have opted for a paper tax return, please submit it by 31st October after the end of the tax year in question. If you opt for online submission you have an extra 3 months to complete your return since the deadline is

    - 31st January after the end of the tax year.

- If filing your return online the first time you are filing your return please register to file your return online. It may take about 2 weeks to get an authentication code, so please leave enough time before the deadline.

- If you fail to file your online return by the 31st January 2016 you may incur fines.

- You can register for self-assessment through the link below. https://www.gov.uk/topic/personal-tax/self-assessment.

- Once you have started to pay tax through self-assessment tax system, you will also have to make "payments on account". These are basically advance payments for the tax you are likely to owe for the current tax year.

- The payments on account are payable to HMRC in two instalments every year, the first on 31 January and the second on the 31st July. Each payment is equal to half the amount of Tax you owe for the previous tax year.

- If you are paying tax through the self-assessment system for the first time, you need to watch out as this might make your first tax bill much bigger than you were expecting.

- For example, if you started your business in October 2016, you would need to complete a self- assessment tax return for the tax year from 6th April 2016 to 5th April 2017. The tax owed for this year would need to be paid to HMRC by 31st January 2018.

- But in addition to your tax bill for 2016/2017, you would also need to pay the first payment on account for the 2017/2018 tax year by the same date.

- It's therefore imperative that you take this into account and put aside enough money to cover your tax bills when they are due. If you are late filing your tax return or paying your tax, HMRC will fine you.

- If you believe your income for the following tax year will be significantly lower, you can apply to HMRC to reduce your payments on account.

How much will your tax bill be?

- For the 2017/18 tax year, the UK personal allowance has been increased to *£11,500.

This is the amount you can earn before paying any income tax at all.

- For income in 2017/18 above this threshold, you will be taxed at the following levels:

    o The Basic Income Tax rate of 20% on income up to *£45,000;

    o The Higher Income Tax rate of 40% on income between £45,001 and £150,000; and

    o The Additional Income Tax rate of 45% on income over £150,000. For the 2017/18 tax year you can therefore earn £56,500 (£11,500 personal allowance plus basic income tax rate threshold of £45,000) before you need to start paying the higher income tax rate of 40%.

- *These figures may change each financial year

National Insurance Contributions (NICs)

- In addition to income tax, as a sole trader, you will also need to make National Insurance Contribution (NICs). The amount you have to pay depends on the level of your earnings.

- There are two types of NICs sole traders have to pay. There are Class 2 NICs – which are currently £2.80 per week (2016/17 Tax Year) – and Class 4 NICs.

- HMRC will work out the amount of Class 4 NICs you are liable for during the annual self-assessment process. It is based on the amount of profit you make, essentially 9% on your earnings between £8,060 and £43,000, and 2% on any profits above this.

Other types of tax – VAT.

- If you are a sole trader, the self-assessment process will take care of most of your tax obligations – it includes details of any income you have received from savings and investments, the disposal of assets, or income from renting out any property you may have.

- If your business has a turnover of more than £83,000 (for the year from April 2016) over a 12 month period, you must also register your business for Value Added Tax (VAT).

- When you are VAT-registered you will need to include VAT to all your bills/invoices. You will also be able to reclaim the VAT you have paid on business costs.

- In some circumstances, it may be beneficial to register your business for VAT, even if your turnover is below the VAT threshold. This is usually the case if the majority of your clients are businesses customers who can reclaim the VAT you charge them. If unsure about dealing with VAT matters, hire an Accountant.

Statutory filings

- If your business is a UK Limited company, after the end of its financial year, your company must prepare:

    o a full statutory annual accounts; and

    o a company Tax return.

- The accounts and tax return has to meet the deadlines for filing with Companies House and HMRC

HMRC and Companies House deadlines

Action	Deadline
File first accounts with Companies	21 months after the date you registered with Companies House
File annual accounts with	9 months after your company's financial year ends
Pay Corporation Tax or tell HMRC	9 months and 1 day after your 'accounting period' for Corporation Tax
File a Company Tax Return	12 months after your accounting period for Corporation Tax ends

*Source

https://www.gov.uk/prepare-file-annual-accounts-for-limited-company/overview

Finding yourself bogged down with the complexities of statutory reporting?

Hire a good Accountant.

F. **Chapter Six - Compliance**

- The law is no respecter of persons! Make sure that you are compliant is all your business operations.

- Keep up-to-date with new regulations and legislation and amendments concerning both the industry you operate in and your statutory obligations

- Ensure you have all the operating licenses you are required to have otherwise you risk being closed down and or given huge fines.

- There are strict requirements on proper record keeping and recording of transactions. Be careful!

G.   Chapter Seven – Accountant

Be very careful.

- Hiring a good Accountant can be expensive but it is invaluable. Hire an Accountant:

    o who believes in the success of your business;

    o who can save you money;

    o who can understand your business and the vision of your business;

    o you can talk to;

    o who is reliable and credible.

- Ask for your Accountant's proof of qualifications. Stay away from bogus Accountants and bookkeepers

- Remember you are paying for the services you are getting, do not be afraid to ask questions and expect answers regarding the services you are being provided.

A positive attitude will go a long way to get you through this Challenging time☺

With this information in your grip, managing your business finances is as simple as ABC

****As simple as A B C ****

www.ingramcontent.com/pod-product-compliance
Lightning Source LLC
Chambersburg PA
CBHW031543210526
45464CB00003B/1128